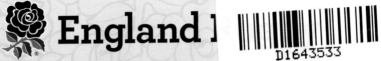

England Rugby

The Official Junior
SUPPORTERS'
Guide

CARLTON KiDS

CONTENTS

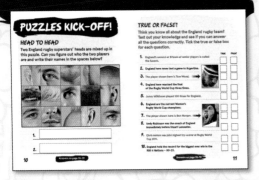

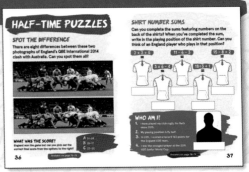

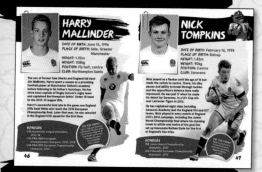

THIS IS ENGLAND!

England is where rugby union began and where all eyes will be come September and October 2015 when the best national teams in the world take part in Rugby World Cup 2015.

This book is packed with profiles of England's leading players both in the senior men's and women's squads as well as the brightest stars in England's Sevens and U20 teams. Explore England's home stadium, Twickenham, try and tackle many different brain-teasing puzzles and prepare for RWC 2015.

SO, LET'S KICK OFF!

The England team sing the national anthem shortly before their QBE International 2014 match against Samoa at Twickenham – the home of English rugby.

Try! Big Ben Morgan roars with delight as he touches down against Australia in 2014. It was one of two tries the number eight scored for England that day.

Mike Brown leaps on the shoulders of (from left to right) Joe Launchbury, Danny Care and Dylan Hartley to celebrate Care's try against Wales in the 2014 RBS 6 Nations.

Ruckley is England's new recruit. He's an all-action English Bulldog with bags of energy who has been appointed England's Ambassador for children's rugby. You can go online and watch videos of him in action at: **www.englandrugby.com/ruckley**

England centre Luther Burrell dives over the try line to score against Wales in the 2014 RBS 6 Nations.

DID YOU KNOW?
England played Scotland in the world's first rugby international all the way back in 1871. Each team played not with 15 but 20 players on the pitch!

ENGLAND'S HOME

Walking into Twickenham Stadium on match day is a breathtaking experience. The noise from the massive crowd can leave your spine tingling, especially when the national anthem is sung or a rousing rendition of *Swing Low Sweet Chariot* – England fans' favourite song – fills the stands.

Twickenham, or 'Twickers' as it is fondly known, has been the Home of England Rugby ever since the national team played their first international match there in 1910. It proved a lucky ground right from the start, with England ending a 12-year losing streak against Wales by winning 11–6. It first held around 12,000 people but has been redeveloped many times and now holds more than 82,000.

DID YOU KNOW?
Twickenham's nickname is the Cabbage Patch due to the fact that the land it is built on was originally farm fields. The Rugby Football Union (RFU) bought the land in 1907 for just £5,500.

Here's the grand view from the South Stand of the Twickenham pitch shortly before England began their QBE International 2014 match against New Zealand.

Inside the England dressing room at Twickenham. On match day, each player has their own named place. You can visit the dressing room on a stadium tour.

Nothing beats the excitement of running onto the pitch surrounded by cheering fans.

MY FIRST MATCH AT TWICKERS!

Date

Score

v

England scorers

Attendance

My Match Rating ★★★★★

Owen Farrell checks out the Fan Wall inside the tunnel which is covered with photos and messages of support sent in by England fans.

PUZZLES KICK-OFF!

HEAD TO HEAD

Two England rugby superstars' heads are mixed up in this puzzle. Can you figure out who the two players are and write their names in the spaces below?

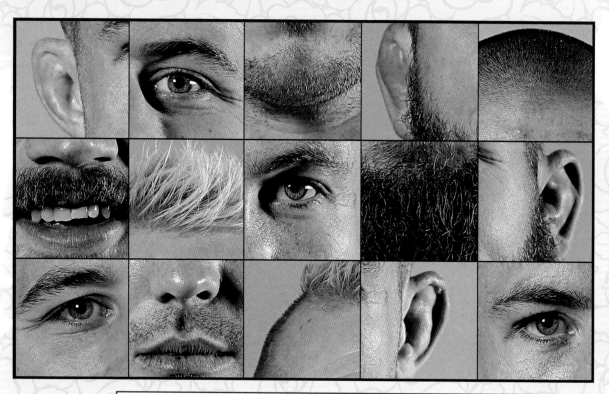

1.

2.

Answers on page 78-79

TRUE OR FALSE?

Think you know all about the England rugby team? Test out your knowledge and see if you can answer all the questions correctly. Tick the true or false box for each question.

		TRUE	FALSE
1.	England's second or B team of senior players is called the Saxons.	✓	✗
2.	England have never lost a game to Argentina.	✓	✗
3.	The player shown here is Tom Wood. ‖➡	✓	✗
4.	England have reached the final of the Rugby World Cup three times.	✓	✗
5.	Jonny Wilkinson played 100 times for England.	✓	✗
6.	England are the current Women's Rugby World Cup champions.	✓	✗
7.	The player shown here is Ben Morgan. ‖➡	✓	✗
8.	Andy Robinson was the coach of England immediately before Stuart Lancaster.	✓	✗
9.	Chris Ashton was joint highest try-scorer at Rugby World Cup 2011.	✓	✗
10.	England hold the record for the biggest ever win in the RBS 6 Nations – 80-23.	✓	✗

Answers on page 78-79

PUZZLES KICK-OFF!

MATCH THE PLAYER

Six top England players have had the letters in their names jumbled up below. Can you unscramble the names and match them to the photographs?

A RED ROOF EGG

B HARSH RIB COWS

C BARN GNOME

D KERB I MOWN

E BANJO CURLY HUE

F SEA OWL CENTURY

Answers on page 78-79

NAME THE OPPONENTS

England have played over 20 different opponents in their rugby history. Can you figure out these seven opponents by looking at their nicknames and their shirt colours?

The Springboks

The Dragons

The All Blacks

The Pumas

The Eagles

The Azzurri

The Wallabies

OPPONENTS QUIZ

Against which team did England score a record 20 tries?

A Uruguay ☐   B The Cook Islands ☐   C Romania ☐

Which team have England played over 130 times, more than any other nation?

A Scotland ☐   B Ireland ☐   C Wales ☐

Answers on page 78–79

13

RECORD BREAKERS

Dazzle your friends and family with these fabulous facts on England's leading record holders.

At the top of the leaderboard for England appearances is **JASON LEONARD**. The prop made his England debut in 1990 and over the next 14 years played an incredible 114 times for England.

LAWRENCE DALLAGLIO played in 28 matches in a row that all ended in wins – the longest winning streak.

BEN YOUNGS was the youngest England scrum half to score a try when he touched down against Australia in 2010. He was 20 years and 287 days old at the time.

14

CHARLIE HODGSON

scored an incredible 44 points in a single game, versus Romania in 2001. Hodgson's big points haul included two tries, two penalty kicks and 14 conversions!

Goal-kicking hero
JONNY WILKINSON

is England's all-time leading points scorer. His 1,179 points included six tries, 239 penalty kicks, 162 conversion kicks and 36 drop goals.

The longest-serving England captain was **WILL CARLING,** who was in charge for 59 matches, winning 44, losing 14 and drawing one.

NICK EASTER

is the oldest try scorer in RBS 6 Nations history. He scored this record try against Italy on February 14, 2015.

OWEN FARRELL

scored the most points (95) in England matches during the year 2014.

DAVE ATTWOOD

England Men's

DATE OF BIRTH: April 5, 1987
PLACE OF BIRTH: Bristol
HEIGHT: 2.01m
WEIGHT: 118kg
POSITION: Lock
CLUB: Bath Rugby

DID YOU KNOW?
Dave has a degree
from Bristol Universi
in Physics and
Philosophy.

Superb in the lineout and strong at restarts, Attwood is an athletic lock who appears all over the pitch. Attwood started his rugby career at Bristol before joining Gloucester in 2009 and then moving on to Bath two years later.

His all-action, driving displays earned him call-ups to the England U19 and U20 teams and in 2010, matches for the England Saxons. In the same year, he debuted for England against New Zealand. He featured strongly in all 11 of England's 2014 matches.

HONOURS
Amlin Challenge Cup runner-up, 2014
Bath Players Player of the Year, 2013

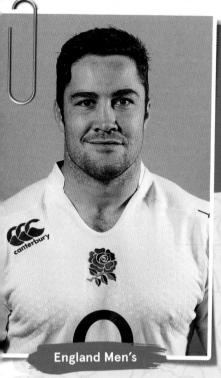

England Men's

BRAD BARRITT

DID YOU KNOW?
While playing rugby, Brad studied part time for an MA in Business at the University of Hertfordshire.

DATE OF BIRTH: August 7, 1986
PLACE OF BIRTH: Durban, South Africa
HEIGHT: 1.86m
WEIGHT: 100kg
POSITION: Centre
CLUB: Saracens

After joining Saracens in 2008, Brad's first England game was for the England Saxons v the United States in the Churchill Cup the following year, where he scored a try. He made his full England debut three years later against Scotland in the RBS 6 Nations and featured in all four games of the QBE Internationals 2012.

Best known for his brave defence and strong tackling, Brad is also a strong and direct attacking runner. His first England points came against New Zealand in the QBE International 2012 when he exchanged passes with Manu Tuilagi to score a memorable try.

HONOURS
British & Irish Lions, 2013
English Premiership champion, 2010–11
English Premiership runner-up, 2013–14

England Men's

MIKE BROWN

DATE OF BIRTH: September 4, 1985
PLACE OF BIRTH: Southampton
HEIGHT: 1.83m
WEIGHT: 92kg
POSITION: Full back
CLUB: Harlequins

Brown joined the Harlequins academy at 15, where he developed into an attacking back. He went on to score 77 tries in his first 230 matches for the Harlequins senior team.

Brave under the high ball in defence and elusive and strong in attack, Brown played some of his early matches on the left wing before settling at full back. He made his England debut against South Africa all the way back in 2007 but cemented his place in the team in 2012.

HONOURS
English Premiership champion, 2011-12
England U21 Six Nations Grand Slam, 2006
Amlin Challenge Cup winner, 2011
Voted RBS 6 Nations player of the championship, 2014

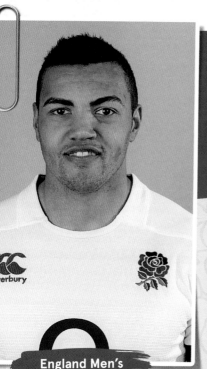

England Men's

LUTHER BURRELL

DATE OF BIRTH: December 6, 1987
PLACE OF BIRTH: Huddersfield
HEIGHT: 1.90m
WEIGHT: 104kg
POSITION: Centre
CLUB: Northampton Saints

A powerful and skilful back, Burrell played his first professional game for Leeds Carnegie aged 19 and completed four seasons at the club before spending a season at Sale Sharks. A move to Northampton Saints came in 2012 and a year later, he was called up into the England senior squad.

The hard-running centre made an instant impact when playing in his first RBS 6 Nations tournament in 2014, scoring three tries in his first four games for England.

HONOURS
Aviva Premiership champion, 2014
Amlin Challenge Cup winner, 2014

DID YOU KNOW?
Luther played for rugby league club Huddersfield Giants before switching to rugby union.

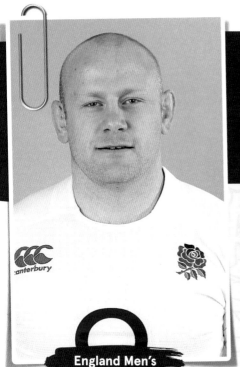
England Men's

DAN COLE

DATE OF BIRTH: May 9, 1987
PLACE OF BIRTH: Leicester
HEIGHT: 1.91m
WEIGHT: 118kg
POSITION: Prop
CLUB: Leicester Tigers

Dan Cole made his England debut against Wales in the 2010 RBS 6 Nations. A strong, solid scrummager and good tackler, he is a major force when the ball is loose and is extremely skilled at getting over the ball in a ruck.

Apart from a loan spell at Bedford, Cole has played all his professional club rugby for his home town team. He also played in 41 out of 42 England matches up to the summer 2013 tour of Argentina and featured in all three British & Irish Lions matches against Australia. He endured a frustrating 2014 when neck surgery kept him out for a spell but roared back at the end of the year.

HONOURS
English Premiership champion, 2009, 2010, 2013
British & Irish Lions, 2013

England Men's

ALEX CORBISIERO

DATE OF BIRTH: August 30, 1988
PLACE OF BIRTH: New York City, USA
HEIGHT: 1.88m
WEIGHT: 116kg
POSITION: Prop
CLUB: Northampton Saints

From early playing days at the London Irish academy, Alex has developed into a powerful and highly skilful prop forward. He played for England U18s and U19s and was part of the England U20 side that reached the final of the 2008 IRB Junior World Championship.

Alex made his debut for the Senior England team in 2011 against Italy. His England career has been interrupted by injuries but when fit and firing, he is one of the most destructive scrummagers in world rugby.

HONOURS

RBS 6 Nations champion, 2011
British & Irish Lions series winner, 2013
English Premiership champion, 2013-14

DID YOU KNOW?
Born to an American-Italian father and with Irish ancestors as well, Alex could have played for Italy, the USA or Ireland but picked England.

21

LEE DICKSON

England Men's

DATE OF BIRTH: March 29, 1985
PLACE OF BIRTH: Verden, Germany
HEIGHT: 1.78m
WEIGHT: 83kg
POSITION: Scrum half
CLUB: Northampton Saints

A busy, bustling scrum half with a slick pass, Lee learned his early rugby at Barnard Castle School in Durham before signing for professional club Newcastle Falcons. He moved to Northampton Saints in 2008 and has since played over 125 English Premiership games for the club, scoring seven tries.

Lee was called up to the England U21 side that won the Grand Slam in 2006, featured for the England Saxons the following year and made his senior debut in England's 13–6 away victory at Murrayfield. He has since featured in more than 15 England senior matches, often coming off the bench.

HONOURS
Aviva Premiership champion, 2014
Amlin Challenge Cup winner, 2009, 2014

DID YOU KNOW?
Lee played for Scotland U19s at the 2004 Junior World Championship but the next year was playing for England U20s.

England Men's

KYLE EASTMOND

DATE OF BIRTH: July 17, 1989
PLACE OF BIRTH: Oldham
HEIGHT: 1.71m
WEIGHT: 82kg
POSITION: Centre
CLUB: Bath Rugby

Kyle began his career in rugby league with St Helens scoring a phenomenal 401 points in 42 games and played four times for the England national team. In 2011, he switched codes and joined Bath in the English Premiership, for whom he has scored more than 10 tries in the English Premiership.

A strong runner who picks clever attacking lines, he is also solid in defence and can kick the ball well. After a series of strong performances, Kyle gained his senior England debut in 2013.

DID YOU KNOW?
Kyle scored his first try for England against Argentina in 2013.

HONOURS
Super League Grand Final runner-up, 2009
Rugby League Four Nations runner-up, 2009

England Men's

OWEN FARRELL

DATE OF BIRTH: September 24, 1991
PLACE OF BIRTH: Wigan
HEIGHT: 1.88m
WEIGHT: 96kg
POSITION: Fly half
CLUB: Saracens

Tough, combative and an aggressive tackler, Farrell is an excellent goal kicker, able to slot the ball over the posts from almost any angle. His accuracy enabled him to score 290 points in his first 30 England matches and 662 points in his first 67 matches for Saracens.

Farrell's father, Andy, played rugby league and rugby union for England and is now England backs coach, while his cousin Liam and uncle Sean also played rugby league for Wigan Warriors.

HONOURS
Shortlisted for IRB World Player
    of the Year, 2012
British & Irish Lions, 2013
English Premiership champion, 2010–11
Heineken Cup runner-up, 2013–14

24

England Men's

GEORGE FORD

DATE OF BIRTH: March 16, 1993
PLACE OF BIRTH: Oldham
HEIGHT: 1.75m
WEIGHT: 84kg
POSITION: Fly half
CLUB: Bath Rugby

A skilful, quick-witted passer and mover of the ball, Ford became the youngest player to make his English professional club debut when he played for Leicester aged 16 years, 237 days. His opponents that day, Leeds Carnegie, featured his older brother Joe.

Ford began playing for England U18s at the age of 15 and has moved rapidly up through the ranks, getting his England senior debut against Wales in the 2014 RBS 6 Nations. At the end of the 2012/13 season he moved from Leicester Tigers to Bath where his father, Mike, is head coach.

HONOURS
IRB U20 Junior World Cup runner-up, 2011
English Premiership champion, 2012-13
LV= Young Player of the Year, 2014

25

COURTNEY LAWES

England Men's

DATE OF BIRTH: February 23, 1989
PLACE OF BIRTH: Hackney, London
HEIGHT: 2.00m
WEIGHT: 111kg
POSITION: Lock, flanker
CLUB: Northampton Saints

Always in the action, Lawes is a fierce tackler, aggressive defender and brilliant lineout jumper. He often puts in man of the match displays for his club and for England having made his international debut in 2009.

He started playing rugby for Northampton Old Scouts rugby club before joining Northampton Saints. Expect to see Lawes all over the pitch making big tackles as well as challenging for the ball in the air and on the ground.

DID YOU KNOW?
Courtney didn't play his first game of rugby until the age of 13. When he first played for Northampton Old Scouts, his position was winger.

HONOURS
IRB Junior World Championship finalist, 2009
Aviva Premiership champion, 2014
Amlin Challenge Cup winner, 2014

England Men's

JONNY MAY

DATE OF BIRTH: April 1, 1990
PLACE OF BIRTH: Swindon
HEIGHT: 1.88m
WEIGHT: 90kg
POSITION: Winger
CLUB: Gloucester Rugby

Seriously quick with a 100m time under 10.7 seconds, May uses his pace to devastating effect in attack. He showed great speed, balance and awareness to score a sensational try against the All Blacks in the QBE International 2014.

May scored a try on his Premiership debut for Gloucester and has since scored more than 45 tries in over 100 games for the West Country club. After playing for the England U20 team, he made his full England debut against Argentina in June 2013.

DID YOU KNOW?
Jonny's debut in the RBS 6 Nations in 2014 against France lasted only eight minutes. He had to leave the field with a broken nose.

HONOURS
Premiership Rugby
Try of the Year, 2012

27

England Men's

CHRIS ROBSHAW

DATE OF BIRTH: June 4, 1986
PLACE OF BIRTH: Redhill
HEIGHT: 1.88m
WEIGHT: 109kg
POSITION: Flanker
CLUB: Harlequins

Often making more tackles than any other player, England's captain is always in the thick of the action. He was made captain of his club in 2010 and just two years later became England skipper in only his second England appearance.

Robshaw captained England in their historic 38-21 win over New Zealand in 2012 and the following year he scored his first try for England during their 20-13 victory over Australia.

HONOURS

English Premiership champion, 2011-12
English Premiership Player of the Year, 2008-09
Amlin Challenge Cup winner, 2011
English Premiership Player of the Year, 2011-12

DID YOU KNOW?
Chris's club Harlequins are based at The Twickenham Stoop, across the road from Twickenham Stadium.

28

England Men's

BILLY TWELVETREES

DATE OF BIRTH: November 15, 1988
PLACE OF BIRTH: Chichester
HEIGHT: 1.91m
WEIGHT: 100kg
POSITION: Centre
CLUB: Gloucester Rugby

A stunning club debut for Bedford in 2008 – when he scored four tries against Manchester – announced Billy as a special talent. Capable of playing fly half but preferring centre, Billy moved to Leicester in 2009, scoring 190 English Premiership points before moving to Gloucester Rugby in 2012.

Billy's all-round performances earned him a call-up to the England Saxons in 2011 and the senior England team in 2013. He obliged with a try on his debut against Scotland in England's 38-13 win and has since scored twice, both against Argentina.

HONOURS
English Premiership champion, 2009-10

DID YOU KNOW?
Billy's nickname is 36, based on his surname being mispronounced as twelve threes – as in 12 x 3!

29

England Men's

BILLY VUNIPOLA

DATE OF BIRTH: November 3, 1992
PLACE OF BIRTH: Sydney, Australia
HEIGHT: 1.88m
WEIGHT: 126kg
POSITION: No.8
CLUB: Saracens

Whether thundering away from the scrum or making a fine tackle, Viliami 'Billy' Vunipola likes to make an impact on the pitch. This was clearly seen on his England debut, when he came off the bench to score a last-minute try against Argentina.

The son of a former Tongan international hooker, Billy was born in Tonga. His family then moved to Britain, where he grew up playing touch rugby with his father, brother Mako and cousins, including Welsh international Toby Faletau. He played two seasons with Wasps before moving to Saracens in 2013.

HONOURS
English Premiership Discovery of the Season award, 2014
Heineken Cup runner-up, 2014

DID YOU KNOW?
In November 2013 Billy started with his brother Mako, and Ben and Tom Youngs. It was the first time in 114 years that two pairs of brothers played for England in the same match.

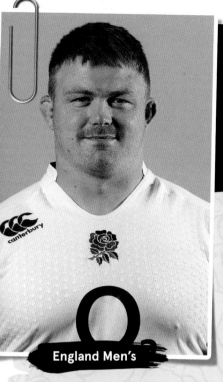

England Men's

DAVID WILSON

DATE OF BIRTH: April 9, 1985
PLACE OF BIRTH: South Shields
HEIGHT: 1.87m
WEIGHT: 122kg
POSITION: Prop
CLUB: Bath Rugby

David was just 18 when he made his English Premiership debut for Newcastle in the front row against the mighty Bath pack, a game that ended in a win for his side. He moved to Bath in 2009 and in October 2014 played his 100th Premiership match for the west country club.

David played for England U19 and U21 sides before finally making his senior debut against Argentina in 2009. A powerful, reliable scrummager, he is also a strong tackler and makes many telling charges with the ball in hand. In the QBE Internationals 2014, he scored his first international try, against South Africa.

DID YOU KNOW?
David made his debut for England at Old Trafford in June 2006. England beat Argentina 37–15.

HONOURS
RBS 6 Nations champion, 2011
England U21 grand slam winner, 2006

31

England Men's

TOM WOOD

DATE OF BIRTH: November 3, 1986
PLACE OF BIRTH: Coventry
HEIGHT: 1.95m
WEIGHT: 107kg
POSITION: Flanker
CLUB: Northampton Saints

Tom is a tough, no-nonsense flanker, good in the lineout and in rucks and defence. He has starred in many stirring England performances including the 38-21 win over New Zealand in 2012, a game in which he was made man of the match.

After recovering from a broken leg, Wood moved from Worcester to New Zealand to play for North Otago for a season, but returned to England in 2010 and was named man of the match in his debut game for Northampton Saints. He captained England on their tour of Argentina in 2013.

HONOURS
English Premiership Player Of The Year, 2010-11
Aviva Premiership champion, 2014
Amlin Challenge Cup winner, 2014

MARLAND YARDE

England Men's

DATE OF BIRTH: April 20, 1992
PLACE OF BIRTH: Castries, St. Lucia
HEIGHT: 1.85m
WEIGHT: 88kg
POSITION: Winger
CLUB: Harlequins

Fast, powerful and an excellent finisher, Marland came to rugby relatively late. Up until the age of 14, he enjoyed athletics and played football as a striker at QPR's Academy. Joining London Irish, he scored a try on his debut in 2010. He also scored a hat-trick of tries for London Irish in his last-but-one game for the club in 2014, before moving to Harlequins for the 2014-15 season.

After scoring nine tries in total for the England U20s, Marland made his full test debut against Argentina in 2013. During the match he scored two tries to help win 51-26, which gave England their first away series win against the Pumas in 32 years.

DID YOU KNOW?
As a teenager, Marland competed in athletics as a triple jumper at the English Schools Championships.

HONOURS
IRB Junior World Championship
    runner-up, 2011
English Premiership Rugby 7s Series
    champion, 2012

England Men's

BEN YOUNGS

DATE OF BIRTH: September 5, 1989
PLACE OF BIRTH: Cawston, Norfolk
HEIGHT: 1.78m
WEIGHT: 92kg
POSITION: Scrum half
CLUB: Leicester Tigers

Quick and probing around the scrum, Youngs became Leicester Tigers' youngest league player when he came off the bench against Bristol in 2007. Having enjoyed spells with the England Sevens and U20 sides, Ben made his debut for England against Scotland in 2010 and made his first start in England's 21-20 victory over Australia later that year.

Since that time, he has been duelling for starts with rivals such as Danny Care and Lee Dickson but has already amassed over 40 caps and six tries. Ben and his older brother Tom became only the fifth set of brothers to start a British & Irish Lions Test match, in 2013.

HONOURS
English Premiership champion, 2009, 2010, 2013
British & Irish Lions, 2013
Leicester Tigers Player of the Season, 2009-10

34

England Men's

TOM YOUNGS

DATE OF BIRTH: January 28, 1987
PLACE OF BIRTH: Norwich
HEIGHT: 1.75m
WEIGHT: 101kg
POSITION: Hooker
CLUB: Leicester Tigers

Tom played as a centre up until 2009 when he switched to being a front row forward. He played some 60 games on loan at Nottingham before returning to Leicester with whom he won the English Premiership in the 2012-13 season.

Assertive and a strong tackler, Tom retains some of his old centre skills in attack where he can be explosive with the ball in hand. He made his senior England debut in the QBE International 2012 against Fiji and appeared alongside his brother, Ben, in England's victory over New Zealand three weeks later. The following year, Tom appeared in all three British & Irish Lions test matches.

HONOURS
British & Irish Lions, 2013
English Premiership
champion, 2012-13

DID YOU KNOW?
Born on a farm in Norfolk, Tom still likes to help out on the farm and has a prized collection of model tractors!

HALF-TIME PUZZLES

SPOT THE DIFFERENCE

There are eight differences between these two photographs of England's QBE International 2014 clash with Australia. Can you spot them all?

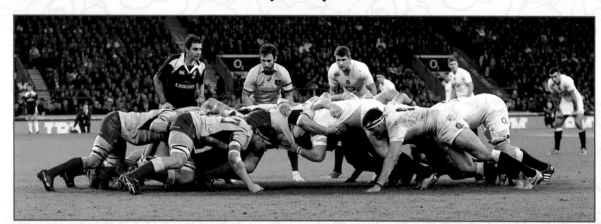

WHAT WAS THE SCORE?

England won the game but can you pick out the correct final score from the options to the right?

A 31-24

B 26-17

C 23-22

Answers on page 78-79

SHIRT NUMBER SUMS

Can you complete the sums featuring numbers on the back of the shirts? When you've completed the sum, write in the playing position of the shirt number. Can you think of an England player who plays in that position?

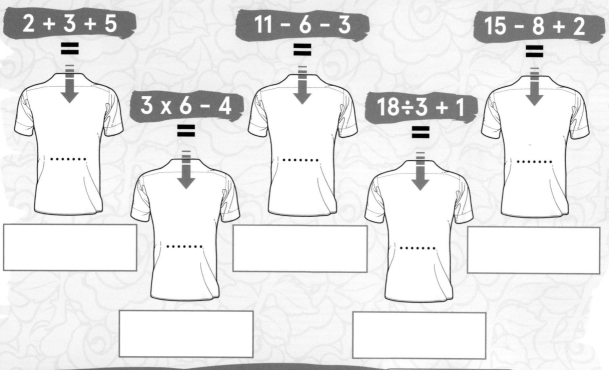

$2 + 3 + 5$ =

$11 - 6 - 3$ =

$15 - 8 + 2$ =

$3 \times 6 - 4$ =

$18 \div 3 + 1$ =

WHO AM I?

1. I have played my club rugby for Bath since 2013.

2. My playing position is fly half.

3. In 2011, I scored a record 143 points for the England U20 team.

4. I was the youngest player at the 2011 U20 Junior World Cup.

Answers on page 78-79

HALF-TIME PUZZLES

It's time for a lineout. Can you match each number in the lineout to a statement on the pitch?

The most points throughout their career scored by an England player.

4

The number of minutes a player spends the field and in the sin bin if shown a yel card by the referee.

The distance in metres between the ground and the top of the crossbar between the goalposts.

76

14

How many different players played for England before Chris Robshaw made his England debut.

59

10

The number of England player who have scored 30 or more tries for their country.

The number of different England players who have scored three tries in a RBS 6 Nations match since Charles Wade was the first in 1882.

1,361

3

The most points England ever conceded in a match.

134

1,179

The most points England scored in a single match.

The most England matches captained by the same player.

38

Answers on page 78-79

SCRUM ANSWERS

Delve into the scrum to pick out the correct answer for each of the questions below. Can you answer all of them correctly?

1. Which England player won a silver medal at the 2006 Commonwealth Games in Rugby Sevens?

2. What is the name of the trophy England and Scotland play for in the RBS 6 Nations?

3. Who was the head coach of the England team when they won Rugby World Cup 2003?

4. Which tank soldier in the Royal Scots Dragoon Guards made his England debut in 2014?

5. Which England player took part in the QBE Internationals 2014 and was England U16 schools discus champion?

6. Who was the coach of the England senior team immediately before Stuart Lancaster?

7. What trophy did the England rugby team lift as winners of Rugby World Cup 2003?

8. Which England player has played for England more than 50 times and for professional clubs in England, France, New Zealand and Japan?

Clive Woodward

James Haskell

The Webb Ellis Cup

The Calcutta Cup

Dave Attwood

Danny Care

Semesa Rokoduguni

Martin Johnson

Answers on page 78-79

England Women's

VICKY FLEETWOOD

DATE OF BIRTH: April 13, 1990
PLACE OF BIRTH: Nuneaton
HEIGHT: 1.62m
WEIGHT: 73kg
POSITION: Hooker
CLUB: Saracens

Fast around the pitch, it is no surprise that Vicky began her rugby career as a centre before moving to hooker in 2008. A month after her switch, she was part of an England U20 pack that pummelled Wales in a 31-0 away win. She made her senior England debut in 2011.

Despite being a young player, Vicky has already notched up over 40 caps for England. She has also played for a variety of clubs including Leicester Forest and Leeds University, where she studied. In 2014 she moved from Lichfield to Saracens, where she won the Women's Premiership in 2014-15.

HONOURS
Rugby World Cup champion, 2014
Women's Six Nations champion, 2012
Women's Premiership champion, 2014-15

DID YOU KNOW?
Vicky was once England's number one-ranked sportswoman at junior level for hurdles.

40

England Women's

KATY MCLEAN

DATE OF BIRTH: December 19, 1985
PLACE OF BIRTH: South Shields
HEIGHT: 1.67m
WEIGHT: 70kg
POSITION: Fly half
CLUB: Darlington Mowden Park Sharks

The inspirational captain of the England women's team, Katy led England to glory at Women's Rugby World Cup 2014. A tough and skilful fly half, she was made captain of England after Women's Rugby World Cup 2010, in which she was England's top scorer.

Katy had juggled playing rugby, including 73 appearances for England, with her job as a primary school teacher. But following the success at the 2014 tournament, she joined other members of the England squad who turned professional, becoming full-time rugby players.

HONOURS

Rugby World Cup champion, 2014
Rugby World Cup runner-up, 2010
Women's Six Nations champion, 2007, 2008, 2009, 2010, 2011, 2012
Awarded an MBE for services to rugby in 2014

41

MARLIE PARKER

England Women's

DATE OF BIRTH: October 2, 1989
PLACE OF BIRTH: Yeovil
HEIGHT: 1.65m
WEIGHT: 73kg
POSITION: Flanker, lock
CLUB: Wasps

When you see how fast Marlie is on the pitch, it is no surprise that the energetic flanker has also played Rugby Sevens for England. Marlie started playing mini rugby at Ivel Barbarians and has since played for Bristol and Bath before joining Wasps in 2013.

At Rugby World Cup 2014, Marlie scored two tries against Spain and followed up with two more tries in just five minutes against Ireland in the semi-final. She was just 24 when she and the rest of the England side were crowned world champions, so you can bet that there's plenty more to come!

HONOURS
Rugby World Cup champion, 2014
Women's Six Nations champion, 2012
England Players' Player of the Six Nations, 2012

42

EMILY SCARRATT

England Women's

DATE OF BIRTH: February 8, 1990
PLACE OF BIRTH: Leicestershire
HEIGHT: 1.81m
WEIGHT: 78kg
POSITION: Centre, full back
CLUB: Lichfield

Emily burst onto the international scene in 2008 with an amazing 12 tries in her first 12 games for England. Comfortable at full back or centre, she also takes kicks for goal and was her team's leading scorer in the 2012 Women's Six Nations.

Emily had an epic Women's Rugby World Cup 2014, scoring two tries, ten penalties and 15 conversions to help propel England to victory and become the tournament's top scorer.

DID YOU KNOW?
Emily was offered a sports scholarship for basketball in the United States when she was 16.

HONOURS
Rugby World Cup champion, 2014
Women's Six Nations champion, 2009, 2010, 2011, 2012
England Women's Rugby Player of the Year, 2013

43

JAMES CHISHOLM

DATE OF BIRTH: August 11, 1995
PLACE OF BIRTH: Haywards Heath
HEIGHT: 1.91m
WEIGHT: 106kg
POSITION: No.8, flanker
CLUB: Harlequins

England U20

James is the younger brother of Harlequins back Ross Chisholm. He played for England U18 and U20 with great success, scoring two tries in the opening game of the 2014 Junior World Championship, which England went on to win.

James is looking to break into the senior Harlequins side. He scored two tries for the club against Newport Gwent Dragons in the 2014 LV= Cup. In the same season, James also appeared for London Scottish.

HONOURS
IRB Junior World Championship
champion, 2014
U18 FIRA/AER European Championship
champion, 2013

DID YOU KNOW?
James was Sussex's U18 high jump champion. His dad Peter managed England's U18 football team and his other brother Ali plays for Esher.

44

England U20

JOEL CONLON

DID YOU KNOW?
Joel made his senior debut for Exeter Chiefs in the LV= Cup in 2012 against London Welsh.

DATE OF BIRTH: May 4, 1994
PLACE OF BIRTH: Taunton
HEIGHT: 1.87m
WEIGHT: 97kg
POSITION: No.8, Flanker
CLUB: Exeter Chiefs

A hot rugby prospect, Joel has already turned heads with his firm tackling and thundering runs for both club and country. He was part of the England U20 squad which won the 2013 Junior World Championship but didn't play in the final. He did, though, play and score a try in one of England's earlier games – a 109-0 thrashing of the USA.

Joel made up for this disappointment the following year when he not only featured in the 2014 final but scored the decisive try of the game as England won narrowly, 21-20 against South Africa.

HONOURS
IRB Junior World Championship
    champion, 2013, 2014
U20 Six Nations champion, 2013
U18 FIRA/AER European Championship
    champion, 2012

45

England U20

HARRY MALLINDER

DATE OF BIRTH: June 13, 1996
PLACE OF BIRTH: Sale, Greater Manchester
HEIGHT: 1.95m
WEIGHT: 108kg
POSITION: Fly half, centre
CLUB: Northampton Saints

The son of former Sale Sharks and England full back Jim Mallinder, Harry spent a season as a promising football player at Manchester United's academy before following in his father's footsteps. He has since been captain of Rugby School's rugby team and captained Northampton Saints' Under 18 team to the 2013-14 league title.

Harry's successful kick late in the game saw England U18s beat Wales and reach the 2014 European Championship final. Later that year, he was selected in the England U20 squad for the first time.

HONOURS
U18 Academies League champion, 2013-14
U18 FIRA/AER European Championship champion, 2013, 2014
U18 FIRA/AER European Championship champion, 2013

DID YOU KNOW?
Harry has just started a Business Studies with Economics degree at The Open University. He has 16 years to complete the course.

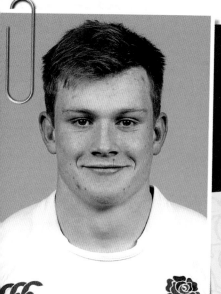

NICK TOMPKINS

DATE OF BIRTH: February 16, 1995
PLACE OF BIRTH: Sidcup
HEIGHT: 1.83m
WEIGHT: 90kg
POSITION: Centre
CLUB: Saracens

England U20

Nick played as a flanker until the age of 16 but made the switch to centre. There, his silky passes and ability to break through tackles and the opposition's defence have really impressed. He was just 17 when he made his debut for Saracens, in a LV= Cup win over Leicester Tigers in 2012.

He has captained eight sides including Saracens Academy and the England U16 and U17 teams. Nick played in every match of England U20's 2014 campaign, including the Junior World Championship final where his stunning break to within one metre of the goal line set up teammate Nathan Earle for the first of England's two tries.

HONOURS
IRB Junior World Championship
    champion, 2014
U18 FIRA/AER European Championship
    champion, 2013

DID YOU KNOW?
Nick scored a try in his first home start for Saracens against Wasps in 2013.

47

England Sevens

CHRISTIAN LEWIS-PRATT

DATE OF BIRTH: December 26, 1990
PLACE OF BIRTH: Richmond
HEIGHT: 1.84m
WEIGHT: 88kg
POSITION: Back

Christian starred for Wellington College at rugby sevens, winning many tournaments including the Rosslyn Park Open in 2009. Turning professional for Northampton, he made his England debut in 2011 at the Dubai Sevens tournament which England won.

On the pitch, Christian is fast, with a good pass and often kicks penalties and conversions for the team. In the 2012-13 season alone, he scored five tries and 70 conversions for England.

DID YOU KNOW?
In the 15-a-side game, Christian made his English Premiership debut in the 2010-11 season for Leeds Carnegie against Gloucester and scored 16 points in the game.

HONOURS
World Cup Sevens runner-up, 2013
Dubai Sevens champion, 2011
Wellington Sevens champion, 2013

TOM MITCHELL

England Sevens

DATE OF BIRTH: July 22, 1989
PLACE OF BIRTH: Cuckfield
HEIGHT: 1.77m
WEIGHT: 86kg
POSITION: Back

Tom made an impact in England Sevens very quickly. In his first game, the former Bristol University and Oxford University student scored with his first touch of the ball against the Cook Islands.

Appointed captain in January 2014, Tom led from the front during the 2013-14 IRB World Sevens Series scoring 358 points, more than any other player. Tom got injured at the 2014 Commonwealth Games tournament but roared back by the end of the year, ready for new challenges.

HONOURS
World Cup Sevens runner-up, 2013
World University Championship
    champion, 2012
Nominated for IRB World Sevens
    Player of the Year, 2014

49

England Sevens

DAN NORTON

DATE OF BIRTH: March 22, 1988
PLACE OF BIRTH: Gloucester
HEIGHT: 1.79m
WEIGHT: 83kg
POSITION: Back

Watch out if Dan has the ball and space to run in. The lightning-fast back raced in to score an incredible 52 tries in a single IRB World Series (2012-13) and has already scored over 170 tries for England's Sevens side.

Dan has played rugby for Moseley, Bristol and Hartpury College and was part of the England U20 team that beat all rivals in the 2008 Six Nations. He is England's second all-time leading try scorer in Sevens and plans on crossing the goal line plenty more times in his career.

HONOURS
World Cup Sevens runner-up, 2013
England Sevens Player of the Year, 2013
Six Nations U20 champion, 2008
Nominated for IRB World Sevens
    Player of the Year, 2013

50

England Sevens

JAMES RODWELL

DATE OF BIRTH: August 23, 1984
PLACE OF BIRTH: Wendover
HEIGHT: 1.93m
WEIGHT: 104kg
POSITION: Forward

A Rugby Sevens powerhouse, James first played for England against the United States in 2008. He has played over 50 international Sevens tournaments in a row for England since.

James began playing rugby at the age of seven for Tring and at Berkhamsted School as a centre or full back. As he grew up and played for teams such as Moseley and England Counties, he played as a lock or number eight.

DID YOU KNOW?
Lawrence Dallaglio is James' biggest rugby hero.

HONOURS
World Cup Sevens runner-up, 2013

MAGGIE ALPHONSI

DATE OF BIRTH: December 20, 1983
PLACE OF BIRTH: Lewisham, London
HEIGHT: 1.63m
WEIGHT: 73kg
POSITION: Flanker
CLUB: Saracens

Dynamic, strong and exciting, Maggie has excited fans of England women's rugby for over a decade, earning 74 caps and appearing in three Rugby World Cup finals, 2006, 2010 and 2014.

She earned the nickname 'Maggie the Machine' for her all-action play, all the more remarkable because she had to overcome being born with a club foot. After England's Rugby World Cup 2014 triumph, Maggie retired from international rugby but continued the season in the Women's Premiership with her club, Saracens.

Legends

HONOURS
Rugby World Cup champion, 2014
Rugby World Cup runner-up, 2006, 2010
Six Nations champion, 2007, 2009, 2010, 2011
Women's Premiership champion, 2014-15
Appointed a Rugby World Cup 2015 Ambassador alongside Jonny Wilkinson and two others.
Awarded an MBE in 2012

GILL BURNS

DATE OF BIRTH: July 12, 1964
PLACE OF BIRTH: Whiston
HEIGHT: 1.80m
WEIGHT: 89kg
POSITION: No.8
CLUB: Waterloo

A natural sportswoman, Gill was picked for British Colleges at basketball, athletics, swimming and hockey. She started playing rugby whilst at Liverpool Polytechnic in 1987. She was selected for England the following year and took part in her first Rugby World Cup in 1991.

In total, Gill played 73 matches for England over a 14 year period and captained England between 1994 and 1999. She led England to their first Rugby World Cup triumph in 1994, retired from international rugby in 2002 but still played some matches for Waterloo until 2013.

Legends

HONOURS
Rugby World Cup winner, 1994
Awarded an MBE in 2005
Voted Waterloo Rugby Club All-Time Hero in 2012
IRB Hall of Fame - Inductee No. 81

WILL CARLING

Legends

DATE OF BIRTH: December 12, 1965
PLACE OF BIRTH: Bradford-on-Avon
HEIGHT: 1.80m
WEIGHT: 90kg
POSITION: Centre
CLUB: Harlequins

Will debuted for England in 1988 at the age of 22 and in the same year was made captain – England's youngest ever. He won his first game in charge, against the world champions, Australia.

Will would captain England during a successful spell that included reaching the final of Rugby World Cup 1991. He played 72 times for England (59 of these as captain) and formed a particularly strong partnership with fellow centre Jeremy Guscott.

HONOURS
Rugby World Cup runner-up, 1991
Five Nations champion, 1991, 1992, 1995, 1996
British & Irish Lions, 1993

54

LAWRENCE DALLAGLIO

Legends

DATE OF BIRTH: August 10, 1972
PLACE OF BIRTH: Shepherds Bush, London
HEIGHT: 1.93m
WEIGHT: 112kg
POSITION: Flanker, No.8
CLUB: Wasps

A powerful, dynamic forward who loved to attack and score tries, Lawrence began his international career in rugby sevens, winning the Sevens World Cup in 1993 with England and debuting for the 15-a-side senior team two years later.

A successful captain for both his beloved club, Wasps, and England, he was the only player to play every minute of England's triumphant 2003 Rugby World Cup campaign. He ended his international career with 85 matches and 85 points from 17 thunderous tries.

DID YOU KNOW?
As a choirboy in the 1980s, Lawrence sang backing vocals on the Tina Turner hit *We Don't Need Another Hero!*

HONOURS
Rugby World Cup champion, 2003
English Premiership champion, 1997, 2003, 2004, 2005, 2008
Five/Six Nations champion, 1996, 2000, 2001, 2003
Heineken Cup champion, 2003–04, 2006–07
British & Irish Lions Series winner, 1997

SUE DAY

Legends

DATE OF BIRTH: October 29, 1972
PLACE OF BIRTH: Watford
HEIGHT: 1.66m
WEIGHT: 70kg
POSITION: Full back, centre, wing
CLUB: Wasps

Sue made her England debut in December 1997 and played for over a decade, scoring 305 points from 59 matches. She appeared at three women's Rugby World Cups in 1998, 2002 and 2006, twice losing in the final to New Zealand.

Sue was still playing for the England Sevens team in 2009, with her last major tournament being the Women's Rugby World Cup Sevens in Dubai. She retired from international rugby that year and from club rugby in 2010.

HONOURS
England's all-time record try-scorer with 65 tries
Women's Rugby World Cup runner-up, 2002, 2006
Six Nations Champion, 2003, 2006, 2007

BEN GOLLINGS

Legends

DID YOU KNOW?
In 2013, Ben coached Sri Lanka's rugby Sevens team.

DATE OF BIRTH: May 13, 1980
PLACE OF BIRTH: Launceston
HEIGHT: 1.75m
WEIGHT: 80kg
POSITION: Back

A true Sevens legend, Ben first played for England Sevens in the 1999–2000 season and never looked back. He scored an incredible 2,652 points in international Sevens rugby, making him the world's all-time leading scorer. That tally included an amazing 220 tries.

Ben also played 15-a-side rugby as a fly half for a wide range of teams including Harlequins, Newcastle Falcons and Worcester Warriors in England, and Gold Coast Breakers in Australia.

HONOURS
Hong Kong Sevens champion, 2003, 2004, 2005, 2006
Commonwealth Games silver medallist, 2006

MARTIN JOHNSON

Legends

DATE OF BIRTH: March 9, 1970
PLACE OF BIRTH: Solihull
HEIGHT: 2.01m
WEIGHT: 119kg
POSITION: Lock
CLUB: Leicester Tigers

The towering captain of England's 2003 Rugby World Cup-winning team was a formidable presence on the pitch. Incredibly strong, he never shied away from confrontation but was also a smart leader on and off the field.

He enjoyed enormous success with the dominant club of his era, Leicester Tigers, and played 84 times for England. He was the only man to captain the British & Irish Lions on two different tours and captained England to 34 wins in 39 matches, an incredible achievement.

HONOURS
Rugby World Cup winner and captain, 2003
Captain of British & Irish Lions 1997, 2001
Premiership champion, 1994–95, 1998–99, 1999–00, 2000–01, 2001–02
Heineken Cup champion, 2001, 2002,
Six Nations Grand Slam winner 1995, 2003
Awarded a CBE in 2004

JASON LEONARD

DATE OF BIRTH: August 14, 1968
PLACE OF BIRTH: Barking, London
HEIGHT: 1.78m
WEIGHT: 111kg
POSITION: Prop
CLUBS: Saracens, Harlequins

Jason was England's youngest ever prop when he made his debut against Argentina in 1990, aged just 21. Months later, he was taking part in his first Rugby World Cup, helping England reach the final for the first time. Jason would appear at four Rugby World Cups in total.

Jason was rock-solid on the pitch, especially in the scrum. He overcame major injuries to play for England a record 114 times and was also picked for three British & Irish Lions tours. Jason will be the president of the Rugby Football Union in season 2015-16.

DID YOU KNOW?
When he first played for England, Jason also had a day job as a plumber!

HONOURS
Rugby World Cup champion, 2003
Rugby World Cup runner-up, 1991
British & Irish Lions Series winner, 1997
Awarded an OBE in 2004

CATHERINE SPENCER

Legends

DATE OF BIRTH: May 25, 1979
PLACE OF BIRTH: Ashford
HEIGHT: 1.79m
WEIGHT: 90kg
POSITION: No.8
CLUBS: Folkestone, Worcester, Bath, Bristol, Aylesford Bulls

Catherine began playing mini rugby at Folkestone at the age of eight. She developed into a powerful player at the back of the scrum and was first capped by England in 2004.

Catherine was made captain of England in 2007, taking the armband from the influential Sue Day and led England to a momentous victory over New Zealand in 2009 as well as a runners-up spot at the Women's Rugby World Cup in 2010.

DID YOU KNOW?
Catherine retired from top flight rugby in 2011 but continued playing for fun at Aylesford Bulls. Her team got promoted twice in two seasons, so Catherine found herself back in the Women's Premiership playing against her old England teammates!

HONOURS
Rugby World Cup runner-up, 2006, 2010
Six Nations champion, 2006, 2007, 2008, 2009, 2010, 2011

JONNY WILKINSON

Legends

DATE OF BIRTH: May 25, 1979
PLACE OF BIRTH: Frimley
HEIGHT: 1.78m
WEIGHT: 89kg
POSITION: Fly half, Centre
CLUBS: Newcastle, Toulon

DID YOU KNOW?
Up until Rugby World Cup 2015, Jonny was the only player to have ever scored points in two Rugby World Cup finals, in 2003 and 2007.

Obsessive with his game, Jonny Wilkinson is England's second most capped player with 91 appearances, the first coming against Ireland in 1998. Forever remembered for kicking the Rugby World Cup-winning drop goal in 2003, those were just three of Jonny's record 277 points in Rugby World Cups. In total, he scored a staggering 1,179 points for England and a further 67 for the British & Irish Lions.

After more than a dozen seasons with Newcastle, Wilkinson moved to France for a fresh challenge. There, he led Toulon to success, winning the Heineken Cup twice and the French league once.

HONOURS
Rugby World Cup winner, 2003
IRB World Player of the Year, 2003
English Premiership champion, 1997-98
Heineken Cup champion, 2013, 2014
RBS 6 Nations champion, 2000, 2001, 2003, 2011
British & Irish Lions, 2001, 2005
Awarded an OBE in 2004

61

CAPS AND POINTS

Find out how many caps England players have played and the points they have scored. A cap is awarded every time a player plays an international test match for their county.

DAVE ATTWOOD
Caps: 17. Points: 0

BRAD BARRITT
Caps: 22. Points: 10

MIKE BROWN
Caps: 34. Points: 30

LUTHER BURRELL
Caps: 8. Points: 15

DAN COLE
Caps: 46. Points: 5

ALEX CORBISIERO
Caps: 19. Points: 0

LEE DICKSON
Caps: 18. Points: 0

KYLE EASTMOND
Caps: 6. Points: 5

OWEN FARRELL
Caps: 29. Points: 290

GEORGE FORD
Caps: 7. Points: 60

COURTNEY LAWES
Caps: 36. Points: 0

JONNY MAY
Caps: 12. Points: 15

CHRIS ROBSHAW
Caps: 33. Points: 10

BILLY TWELVETREES
Caps: 17. Points: 15

BILLY VUNIPOLA
Caps: 13. Points: 10

DAVID WILSON
Caps: 41. Points: 5

All figures correct up to 1st March 2015.

TOM WOOD
Caps: 34. Points: 0

MARLAND YARDE
Caps: 7. Points: 20

BEN YOUNGS
Caps: 43. Points: 35

TOM YOUNGS
Caps: 18. Points: 0

VICKY FLEETWOOD
Caps: 48. Points: 10

KATY MCLEAN
Caps: 75. Points: 392

MARLIE PACKER
Caps: 32. Points: 40

EMILY SCARRATT
Caps: 55. Points: 301

MAGGIE ALPHONSI
Caps: 74. Points: 140

GILL BURNS
Caps: 73. Points: unknown

WILL CARLING
Caps: 72. Points: 54

LAWRENCE DALLAGLIO
Caps: 85. Points: 85

SUE DAY
Caps: 59. Points: 230

BEN GOLLINGS
Caps: 70. Points: 2,652

MARTIN JOHNSON
Caps: 84. Points: 10

JASON LEONARD
Caps: 114. Points: 5

CATHERINE SPENCER
Caps: 63. Points: 90

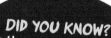
JONNY WILKINSON
Caps: 91. Points: 1,179

DID YOU KNOW?
On the occasion of their first match for England a player is presented with an actual cap to wear. The cap below was given to a player in the very first England team in 1871; this cap can be seen in the World Rugby Museum at Twickenham.

MY ENGLAND DREAM TEAM

Now you know all about England rugby's top players of today and yesterday, it's your turn to step into the head coach's shoes and create your own match day squad.

Choose any player you like when building your very own dream team. Your side can include top players of the present or past and even you, your family and friends! Choose who you would make captain.

PLAYER POSITIONS

1. Loose-head prop

2. Hooker

3. Tight-head prop

4. Lock

5. Lock

6. Blind-side flanker

7. Open-side flanker

8. No.8

9. Scrum half

10. Fly half

11. Left wing

12. Inside centre

13. Outside centre

14. Right wing

15. Full back

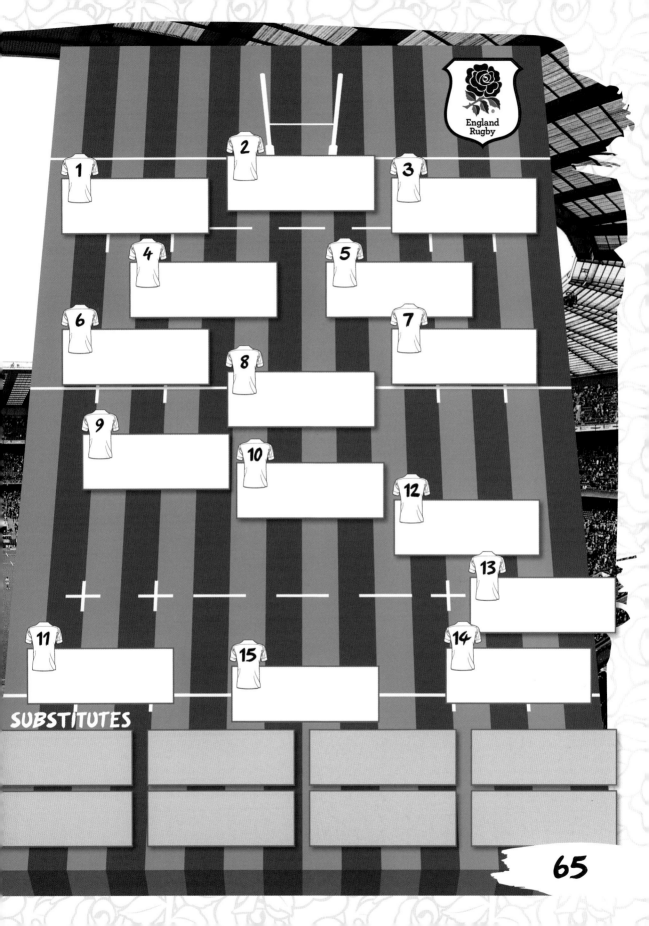

SUBSTITUTES

65

FULL-TIME PUZZLES

SPOT THE BALL

Take a look at this photo of England playing New Zealand in 2014. Circle the place where you think the ball is.

SPOT THE PLAYERS

Tick the box of any England players you can see in the picture.

☐ Tom Wood   ☐ Ben Youngs   ☐ Johnny May   ☐ Dave Attwood

66

Answers on page 78-79

MEMORY TEST

Just how good is your memory? Give it a proper workout with this brainbusting puzzle. Study everything on this page for two minutes then turn over the page. See how many questions you can answer.

Answers on page 78-79

FULL-TIME PUZZLES

MEMORY TEST QUESTIONS

How much can you remember? It's time to test your memory.

1. What object was in the top right-hand corner?

2. What was England women's captain Katy McLean holding?

3. What item of protection is between the goalposts?

4. How many rugby balls were there?

5. Which shirt number was upside down?

6. Who was the player kicking the ball?

7. How many kicking tees were there?

8. What colour tracksuit top was Chris Robshaw wearing?

WHO AM I?

1. I have played all my adult rugby for Harlequins.

2. I play at full back but have also played for England ten times as a winger.

3. I scored two tries against Italy in the 2014 RBS 6 Nations tournament.

4. My surname is the name of a colour.

Answers on page 78-79

TRY HARD

Can you add up the number of points scored from these tries, conversions and penalty kicks? When you think you have the right answer, write them in the scoreboard on the right.

TRY = 5 PTS • **CONVERSION** = 2 PTS • **PENALTY KICK** = 3 PTS

a) 3 TRIES +
   2 CONVERSIONS +
   0 PENALTY KICKS =

B) 1 TRY +
   1 CONVERSION +
   6 PENALTY KICKS =

C) 5 TRIES +
   4 CONVERSIONS +
   2 PENALTY KICKS =

D) 7 TRIES +
   7 CONVERSIONS +
   4 PENALTY KICKS =

Answers on page 78-79

MEMORABLE MATCHES

Let's look back at some magical matches featuring amazing England performances from the Senior Men's, Women's and U20 squads in the past decade.

WORLD CUP WINNERS

DATE: November 22, 2003
SCORE: Australia 17–20 England
COMPETITION: Rugby World Cup 2003
TEAM: Senior England Men

An incredibly tight, tense final saw Jason Robinson score a try for England but Elton Flatley tie the scores in the 80th minute to take the match into 20 minutes of extra time. With less than a minute left, Jonny Wilkinson scored the drop goal that made England champions.

SCRUMMAGING SUCCESS

DATE: October 6, 2007
SCORE: Australia 10–12 England
COMPETITION: Rugby World Cup 2007
TEAM: Senior England Men

England met Australia at the next Rugby World Cup, this time at the quarter final stage. A powerful England scrum overpowered the Australian forwards and Jonny Wilkinson kicked four penalties to take England into the semi-finals.

ENGLAND DEFEAT THE ALL BLACKS

DATE: December 1, 2012
SCORE: England 38–21 New Zealand
COMPETITION: QBE Internationals
TEAM: Senior England Men

The All Blacks were the number-one team in the world when they played at Twickenham. Leading 12–0 at half time, England had to defend against an early second-half comeback from New Zealand, before tries from Brad Barritt, Chris Ashton and Manu Tuilagi saw them score the most points they'd ever achieved against New Zealand in an epic win.

MEMORABLE MATCHES 2

WOMEN'S WORLD CHAMPIONS

DATE: August 17, 2014
SCORE: England 21–9 Canada
COMPETITION: Women's Rugby World Cup
TEAM: England Women

Danielle Waterman scored England's first try in the 33rd minute and Emily Scarratt sealed a famous win with England's second try in the 74th minute. In addition, Scarratt kicked one conversion and three penalties leading England to win the Women's Rugby World Cup for the first time since 1994.

JUNIOR GIANTS

DATE: June 20, 2014
SCORE: England 21–20 South Africa
COMPETITION: IRB Junior World Championship
TEAM: England U20s

After crushing Ireland 42–15 in the semi-finals, England found themselves 10–3 down after 19 minutes of the final. They rallied superbly with tries from Nathan Earle and replacement Joel Conlon to lead early in the second half. They showed strong defence to hold out against the 2012 World Champions and win the championship for the second year in a row.

OVERPOWERING THE PUMAS

DATE: June 15, 2013
SCORE: Argentina 26–51 England
COMPETITION: Two Test Series
TEAM: Senior England Men

With 13 England players away with the British & Irish Lions, a new look England team with lots of young players put in a great performance which saw Marland Yarde score two tries on his debut. The victory saw England clinch their first away series win against Argentina in 32 years.

MEET THE BOSS!

Stuart Lancaster was appointed England's permanent head coach in 2012. He has led England to four runners-up finishes in a row in the RBS 6 Nations and epic wins over southern hemisphere giants New Zealand and Australia.

Stuart was once a PE teacher at Kettlethorpe High School in Wakefield but also spent nine seasons playing rugby union as a flanker for Leeds Carnegie. After retiring from playing in 2000, he began coaching at Leeds Carnegie and became Director of Rugby there in 2005.

DID YOU KNOW?
Stuart was an all-round sportsman at school who scored centuries at cricket and started out playing rugby as a hooker.

COACH PROFILE

DATE OF BIRTH: October 9, 1969
PLACE OF BIRTH: Penrith, Cumbria
NATIONALITY: English

Playing and Coaching Career
1992-2000 Player - Leeds
2001-2006 Head of Leeds Academy,
2005-2007 Director of Rugby, Leeds Carnegie
2007-2011 Head of RFU Elite Player Development
2012   Appointed permanent head coach of England

Stuart giving instructions during an England training camp.

Holding the Cook Cup after England beat Australia in 2014. Stuart is surrounded by his coaching team.

He then joined the Rugby Football Union's (RFU) as Head of Elite Player Development and took charge of the England Saxons team as head coach. During Stuart's reign, the England Under-20 team reached three out of four IRB Junior World Championship finals (2008, 2009 and 2011).

Stuart took charge of an England team that had disappointed fans with an early exit from Rugby World Cup 2011. He has restored pride in their play and given debuts to lots of exciting new players from thundering forwards Ben Morgan and Joe Launchbury to young backs such as George Ford and Jonny May.

Stuart applauds the Twickenham crowd after England finish runners up in the 2014 RBS 6 Nations Championship.

ROAD TO RWC 2015

The countdown is well under way to the biggest rugby competition in the world – Rugby World Cup 2015. Excitement mounts the closer the calendar gets to September 18, 2015 – when RWC 2015 kicks off with England playing Fiji in the opening match.

AUTUMN ACTION

England began their year-long build-up to RWC 2015 with a summer tour to New Zealand followed by a series of four QBE Internationals 2014 matches, all against southern hemisphere opponents. Narrow defeats to South Africa and New Zealand were disappointing but England rallied to defeat Samoa and old foes, Australia.

George Ford and Chris Robshaw tackle Australian player Rob Horne during the Autumn Internationals 2014. England beat Australia 26-17.

ROPHY TOUR

While England train, the ltimate prize in world rugby, he Webb Ellis Trophy travelled round the world. Starting May 2014 in Japan it visited a range of countries including Australia, China, the US and Madagascar. It completed its world tour in France in May 2015.

England's forwards practice their scrummaging during an England training camp.

TRAINING CAMPS

In between playing for their clubs and representing their country, the England squad gathers for training camps. Under the eye of Stuart Lancaster and his coaching team, England work on their skills and tactics.

SIX NATIONS 2015

England's last competitive tournament before RWC 2015 was the 2015 RBS 6 Nations. It kicked off on a Friday night in early February with England playing Wales at Cardiff's Millennium Stadium. It's an important test for the team heading towards RWC 2015 with players looking to impress the coaches and excite and entertain fans.

Stuart Lancaster and his coaching team will have lots of decisions to make in the run up to the start of Rugby World Cup 2015.

England Rugby

ANSWERS

PAGE 10 - **HEAD TO HEAD**

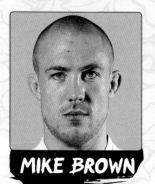

MIKE BROWN

JOE MARLER

PAGE 11 - **TRUE OR FALSE?**

1.......... ✓ ☐   6.......... ✓ ☐
2.......... ☐ ✗   7.......... ✓ ☐
3.......... ☐ ✗   8.......... ☐ ✗
4.......... ✓ ☐   9.......... ✓ ☐
5.......... ☐ ✗   10........ ✓ ☐

PAGE 12 - **MATCH THE PLAYER**

 B
 A
 D
 E
 F
 C

PAGE 13 - **NAME THE OPPONENTS**

The Springboks: SOUTH AFRICA

The Dragons: WALES

The All Blacks: NEW ZEALAND

The Pumas: ARGENTINA

The Eagles: USA

The Azzurri: ITALY

The Wallabies: AUSTRALIA

PAGE 13 - **OPPONENTS QUIZ**

Against which team did England score a record 20 tries?
C Romania
Which team have England played 133 times, more than any other nation?
A Scotland

PAGE 36 - **SPOT THE DIFFERENCE**

78